You British

Allow an au-pair into your house and you're letting yourself in for more than broken English and broken dishes. Even in an age of eminent Victorians, no Englishman was a hero to his valet. Today's au-pairs are a fresh young generation of caustic observers from across the seas, of the Englishman's foibles. How do the English rate in their eyes?

Rosanna from Italy thinks everyone in England is a hypocrite except for George Brown. Dominique from France thinks our meal-times are 'a terrible murder three times a day'. Julie from America is sure we're not really animal lovers – 'just people lovers gone wrong'. Our boys, it is agreed, are dirty, sex-mad and sometimes 'very very nice like Prince Philip'. Our girls, believe it or not, sometimes 'don't wear any underwear' – ('it is not like that in my country,' says Mashie from Yugoslavia). At Christmas we gobble like pigs and in the summer we make love in the parks. Otherwise we are merely 'stiff and strange all year long'.

Here, anatomized, is the bizarre life-style of the English middle classes; annotated by that traitor in our midst, Mark Boxer, with a selection of deadly cartoons featuring those slave-drivers of NW1.

You British

as the au-pair girls see us

ELAINE GRAND

drawings by Marc

Weidenfeld and Nicolson 5 Winsley Street London W1

SBN 297 00216 3

Printed in Great Britain by Bristol Typesetting Co Ltd
Barton Manor, St Philips, Bristol

A t any given time there are over thirty thousand au-pair girls living in Great Britain. These are the girls who come here from all over the world (but usually from

The Rise and Fall of an au-pair

First meeting: at Victoria Station. The parcel contains presents for the children. Pleases her employers enormously when she asks for nearest catholic church. Fail to spot her disappointment on discovering it's within three miles

the Continent) to study the English language, and to live with an English family.

The au-pair idea originated in pre-war years. At that time it conformed to the literal meaning of ' au-pair ' – ' on the same level '. Well-to-do middle-class families sent their eighteen-year-old daughters to live with a Continental family for a year, ostensibly in order to study the customs, culture, and language of a foreign country. In return, the foreign family often sent *their* daughter to stay with the English parents of *their* au-pair. It was all very social and civilized, and served as a kind of finishing school for the girls themselves.

First doubts:
au pair starts
noticing high
nutritional value
of food given to
the dog in comparison
to high starch content
of her evening meal.
excused on the
grounds that "those
continentals are
only used to
pasta, aren't they"

Now, with the decline in number of full-time domestic servants, and with the growth of the 'new' middle-classes, a different kind of au-pair has emerged. She is still supposed to spend her time here as a serious student of the English language (and a few of them actually do), but, in fact, she has become a source of cheap domestic labour. Despite the fact that the Home Office implores the employer in an official pamphlet to 'treat the au-pair as a member of your family. She should be required to do no more work than the daughter of the house would normally do', the au-pair often finds she is treated as an under-paid skivvy. To be fair, there are some au-pairs whose motives for coming here are much more bizarre than a simple desire to master the language, and

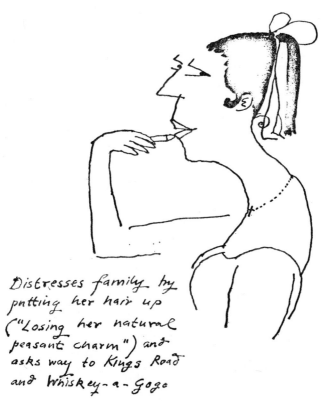

Distresses family by putting her hair up ("Losing her natural peasant charm") and asks way to Kings Road and Whiskey-a-gogo

in those cases it is the employers who end up feeling like exploited innocents.

Every au-pair has one great advantage over other visitors to this country. She is actually *living* with us. The tourist is apt to see only the façade of a country, the grand occasions, the historic monuments, the expensive restaurants, the luxury hotels. Not the au-pair. She lives with us, eats with us, works with us, talks with us (and yes, in some cases, sleeps with us). She is a constant observer, both outside and *inside* the home.

So that's the idea of this book. To find out what some of these thirty thousand daughters honestly think of us.

after weeks of procastination mistress of the house asks au pair to clear out children's play room that has been untouched by human hand for several years. au pair decides Victorians idea of work she learnt as a student is all wrong. Decides it is Nasty, Brutish and Long ..

8

I contacted au-pairs through ads in personal columns, language-school notice boards, employment agencies, and posted questionnaires. But the final selection of fourteen girls was quite arbitrary on my part, and not based on any scientific method known to man or sociologist. It was simply due to the fact that all these girls had definite opinions and weren't

First major row: an Indian student discovered by master of the house making way to upper attic where up till now au pair was thought to lead blameless life.

afraid to voice them. Of course the au-pair herself is not an
'average' girl. She is more adventuresome, more mature,
more confident than the majority of her contemporaries. She
has to be able to launch herself into a completely untried and
completely foreign environment. But, despite the un-scientific
approach, despite the lack of 'random sampling', the virtual
unanimity of opinion amongst these girls from fourteen different countries makes me think that they may indeed be truly
representative of the other twenty-nine thousand, nine hun-
dred and eighty-six.

Between them they have spent over twenty-two years here.

Having asked for address of
dearest doctor, employers
panic

Most of their opinions are based upon life as it is lived in London and its surrounding suburbs by middle-class families. So for the word 'English' in this book, I think one should mentally add, 'big city, middle-class'. I suppose the overall impression given is that they don't like us. But it is much easier to criticize than to compliment, particularly in a foreign language. Basically I think they must have a sneaking fondness for us, otherwise they would all have rushed back home years ago. At the back of the book I have given quick descriptions of the girls themselves. The girls are real, but the names aren't.

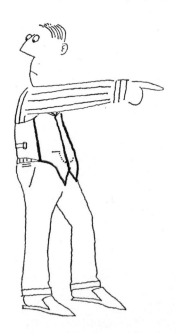

'The Englishman is still a colonist, so now that
he has no colonies he colonizes his women'

JULIE: (*American*)

When you look at this country on a map, or from a plane, all you can see is this little crumb floating around somewhere in the North Sea. Yet it has an ego bigger than the Pacific Ocean. They are convinced that they are GREAT Britain. Still yet. And no one, but no one will *un*-convince them.

DOMINIQUE: (*French*)

The English man is still a colonist, so now that he has no colonies he colonizes his women. He takes over this strange country, this female, he protects it, manages it, supplies it. They must be taken care of, but also show a profit. I suppose the children and the bed are the profit. But the woman is feeling like the colonies did, she doesn't feel she belongs to anyone any more, she just feels lonely and exploited.

ROSANNA: (*Italian*)

Everyone in England is a hypocrite except for George Brown.

CATHERINE: (*Dutch*)

You are so poor, you are so awful, you are so reserved, you are so dull, and yet every young person in the world wants to come here. That is *really* peculiar.

MARLENE: (*German*)

I was surprised to find that there are so many rich people in this country, because in our papers for many years, we have read that you were very very poor, but everyone seems quite rich here . . . most people, anyway, and it's not what I thought.

LENA: (*Polish*)

You can't easy tell who is the Jews here.

EVA: (*Danish*)

The English honestly still think of all foreigners as bloody wogs.

CARMEN: (*Spanish*)

The higher you go the dirtier the English are . . . and I don't mean untidy, I mean truly dirty.

MARLENE: (*German*)

The butchers' shops are disgusting. Flies fly around and land on the meat, and everything smells of blood and dirt. I prefer to buy my meat wrapped up and hygienic in a department store, but the English like to get their meat naked and bloody. I think this is an odd prejudice.

ROSANNA: (*Italian*)

All the women have shaved under the arms.

DOMINIQUE: (*French*)

They are in fashion but they have no elegance.

ROSANNA: (*Italian*)

They often wear dirty underwear.

MASHIE: (*Yugoslavian*)

Sometimes the women here don't wear *any* underwear. It is not like that in my country.

KARIN: (*Norwegian*)

Then once they are married they say 'Oh well, it's over, I am married, I can relax now', and they even let themselves go physically, and they seem to take it for granted that their husbands will be unfaithful to them.

CATHERINE: (*Dutch*)

Years ago young people wanted to be in Paris, in New York, but now it is London, because London is the centre of the world. No, it is not really the centre of the world, it is the centre of the *attention* of the world.

EVA: (*Danish*)

London doesn't swing, it's in orbit. Everybody gambles, they are just taking it for granted. Like breathing, like sleeping, it is necessary to gamble.

INGRID: (*Swedish*)

Striptease clubs at *lunch time*.

CLAUDE: (*Belgian*)

Women smoking on the streets.

Mashie: (*Yugoslavian*)

I have been to Carnaby Street and I like very much. Is like Christmas there all year round. But is to look there, not to buy there, because looking is cost nothing, but the clothes cost quite a lot I think, and are not for wearing but to take home and hang in the pantry because if you wear these clothes they are all coming apart on your body.

Lili: (*Austrian*)

I don't think that any city has as many night clubs as London. Well, what they *call* night clubs. Not that they are very glamorous. They all seem to be small dark places with lots of back doors with stairs that go up to rooms for some etcetera. And of course it's exciting to these little girls who come from boarding schools or convents. They want to explore, don't they? So they do. If they're strong enough or lucky enough they get through all right. But some don't. You see a lot of girls go to Soho at night hoping that something *will* happen to them. Yet they are also hoping that they will just manage to escape. But *only* just.

Marianne: (*Swiss*)

You see men buying sweets and chocolates . . . pounds of them . . . really . . . and you think they are buying them for the children. When they leave the shop you see it is the men who are eating them all up. Nowhere have I seen men, grown men, eating sweets like this.

Lili: (*Austrian*)

Cooking? Well, one roast for the weekend and it's got to last the whole week with a lot of sausages. And lots of cabbages and lots of peas of course. Maybe as a treat fish fingers.

MARIANNE: (*Swiss*)

Really the English cook relies on two things to cover up all the mistakes and all the lack of variety in the food. Custard and gravy. CUSTARD AND GRAVY. Everything, everything is swimming in them, and I don't think they would notice if they had custard on their potatoes and gravy on their pudding. The whole idea is *not* to notice what you're eating.

ROSANNA: (*Italian*)

They are stiff and strange all year round.

JULIE: (*American*)

Well you've got to learn that if they say to you ' You must drop in and see us someday' the *last* thing they want in the world is for you ' to drop in and visit them someday '. I know, I've had some pretty glassy-eyed receptions. But I've got the picture now, you just lie back and say ' I'd love to ' and they know *you're* lying and you know *they* know you're lying and it's all very polite.

ROSANNA: (*Italian*)

Then at Christmas they go mad, they go like pigs. They starve all year around, they don't have a friend for a drink all the year around, then at Christmas they are all like pigs, literally like pigs at bowls. The first time I saw a country Christmas I was *terrified*! You know they start saving around June or July so that two days before Christmas this big box of whisky can be brought into the house, and it is gone by Boxing Day. People who don't drink all year round drinking a full bottle of whisky in one night. And suddenly they are friendly . . . *so* friendly. ' Eat eat ', ' Drink drink ', they say, ' It is Christmas '. No, it is *not* Christmas, this English Christmas, it is just like pigs who have been waiting all year for their trough. Then the next day they go back to being stiff and strange.

MARIANNE: (*Swiss*)

The most peculiar thing is to see the husband and wife spending their whole evening at the pub. And they just sit there all evening, and the husband plays darts, and the wife just sits with other women, and no one really talks, they just drink, and I think to myself . . . 'Oh God, where is the home, where is the love, where is the family?'

MARLENE: (*German*)

When they are young the men are all right, they are ambitious, they work hard. Then as soon as he marries he gets lazy. He just wants to be at home and he doesn't care about anything else. Every Monday morning he says 'Oh dear, I wish it was next Friday', and he just lives for his weekend when he can just sit and do nothing but watch television. Maybe this is his idea of what his life should be, to get through the week just hating every day, so he can watch television all Saturday and Sunday. It is not like this in Germany.

ROSANNA: (*Italian*)

Central London is exciting only because ninety-five per cent there is foreigners.

LENA: (*Polish*)

You say you are tolerant but I don't think this is really so. You just use the black people who come here, use them to do all the hard work, but you don't really like these black people, you just use them.

MARLENE: (*German*)

The situation of the country could be better if things were not so free. In every country the Government must change some things sometimes but this is very hard in England. No matter what the Government wants to do everyone starts shouting 'No you can't do that, you are taking away our freedom'. And I think maybe sometimes you must let the Government go ahead and change things.

DOMINIQUE: (*French*)

They will take all the bad things from America, but not the good things like central heating, because they think 'Ohhh we will get so used to all these good American things that we will need them all the time and then we will be an American state'. So they go cold in the winter while they are watching American TV.

EVA: (*Danish*)

I used to feel sorry for them and think maybe they were too poor to afford central heating. But now I know they *prefer* to freeze, because they are basically still a warrior race, and they are frightened that too much comfort will get them soft.

JULIE: (*American*)

Well, they've got this pathetic belief that God, the Gulf Stream and two lumps of coal will keep them warm.

EVA: (*Danish*)

I don't think you look upon your children as just children, but as future conquerors, because for so many generations you have been brought up to conquer. Of course now you have nothing left to conquer, but you still bring your children up in the same way. What you should do is put a great big black cross over everything in your past, as far as bringing up children goes I mean, and then say to yourselves, and to these children 'Right, we will start from Chapter One. And this Chapter One has never been used before'. And I think until you do this they will grow up disappointed because they will discover for themselves that the English are no longer conquerors. I am sorry, but that is true.

Marlene: (*German*)

An English man and a German girl together would be good parents. But it wouldn't work the other way around, because an English mother is never strict enough and a German father is maybe too strict. So a German mother with an English father, they would make perfect children I think.

Dominique: (*French*)

I think to be married to an English man would be very boring. There would be nothing to make you excited that he is coming home to you each evening. He just walks in and says 'Hello', then he sits down and eats. He never brings flowers or a bottle of wine. He does not care what he eats, so his wife does not care to make the food interesting, so they just sit and eat everything up.

Marlene: (*German*)

They treat their animals the same way as they treat their children. They even talk to them the same way, 'Now sir', 'Silly boy', 'Come along darling', 'You silly little girl', and you never know whether they are talking to the dog or the child.

'They treat their animals the same way as they treat their children'

JULIE: (*American*)

I don't think they're really *animal* lovers, I think they're just people lovers gone wrong.

CATHERINE: (*Dutch*)

Once I was in a family that had a very vicious dog, and one day when they had left me alone in the house, the dog bit the child. The child was just two and he was bleeding and I was terribly upset about this. So I said to the parents 'Look, do you want your child to be bitten to death one day? You must do something'. The father's mother had a big house in the country so I said 'Send him away to your mother's house in the country, he will be happier there, but if you don't I will not stay here any longer'. So they told me they would think about it, and I could see they were very upset. And they discussed it for days and days, and then they came to me and they said 'No, you will have to leave, because we have decided we cannot think of sending him away to the country'. I said 'All right, but you are crazy, that crazy dog would be better off in the country' and they looked at each other and they said 'The dog! We thought you meant the baby!'

EVA: (*Danish*)

They worry about old donkeys in Algeria but they let their own horses and ponies be eaten on the Continent.

INGRID: (*Swedish*)

The English sense of humour is very funny . . . I don't understand it.

CARMEN: (*Spanish*)

In one house I worked where the dog and I got the scraps left over from the dinner table, that's what we ate, but the dog got more than I did.

ROSANNA: (*Italian*)

The usual family dinner here is roast beef cut so thin you can see right through it to the pattern on your plate. Okay. In Italy we put the meat in the middle and you can cut the slice yourself, take what you want. But okay, maybe it is more polite to cut these thin slices. But I think it is terrible about the potatoes. The English are always complaining that all we ever eat is pasta. But here, you are given roast potatoes, mashed potatoes, and boiled potatoes. Yes, roast potatoes, *and* mashed potatoes, *and* boiled potatoes . . . *all together*! And yet they will complain about our pasta. God!

CLAUDE: (*Belgian*)

When an Englishman speaks a foreign language he thinks it is very funny. They think it is a big joke that there *is* another language. They only take English seriously and all the other languages are just to laugh at, not to speak with.

LILI: (*Austrian*)

On the whole I think it is best if the English folk stay on their little island. They do not really want to change, to understand other folk, to jump in the big pond, to take any risk.

MARLENE: (*German*)

It is not good to say you are German to bus conductors, they are inclined to think a bit bad of all Germans.

CLAUDE: (*Belgian*)

The reason Englishmen is so conservative is that they love old things and they will pay a lot of money for antiques and they are not really worth much because a lot of these antiques are very old.

JULIE: (*American*)

We are always accused of being a materialist nation but the worst examples of materialism I have ever seen are right here. You take a suburban Sunday and what do you see? Every man is out in front of his house washing and polishing his car, he is positively *cherishing* it. You get the feeling that that car is the only material possession he has in the world and by God he's going to hang on to it. Back home we are not as obsessed by this *permanent* material possession as you are. Maybe the English can't afford obsolescence, but I think this clinging to material things is really a part of their character. Old houses, old cars, old clothes, old anything, they won't destroy them because they'd feel they were destroying part of themselves.

LENA: (*Polish*)

I think it is a good idea to have a Queen. She *seems* nice, but I was told she had Jewish blood in her.

KARIN: (*Norwegian*)

I am wearing very odd clothes at some times, and people hardly look at you, and that is good. But, on the other hand, if you lie in the gutter, dying or drunk or sick, they won't look either you see. That is their idea of politeness. But sometimes in some ways you want someone to take notice of you, someone to help you.

INGRID: (*Swedish*)

When I first came over I knew that Scandinavian girls had a

very bad reputation sexually – or a very good one, depending on whose point of view you speak from. But I was surprised to see how promiscuous the English girl was. Not only are they doing it all the time, they are talking about it all the time. Whether they're enjoying the doing I'm not so sure, I think maybe they are enjoying more the talking *about* than the doing.

ROSANNA: (*Italian*)

When I first saw the way they acted in Italy I said, ' Oh well, they are on holiday, let them go a bit wild ', but now I see they are like this all the year round.

JULIE: (*American*)

They certainly don't have much in common with Julie Andrews, do they?

MARIANNE: (*Swiss*)

Some of them are just bouncing from man to man and they are almost in a state of madness. In other countries boys and girls, men and women, can be friends, just friends. But here it seems it is sex, marriage, or nothing. Nothing at all, no genuine relationship, which is very bad for the girl. And a lot of young men don't seem even interested in girls. I see them at dances and clubs, hundreds of them just standing around, not looking at the girls, only interested in each other. I don't know if they are homosexual, maybe they don't have enough money to spend on girls. But there aren't enough men interested in girls to match up with all the girls who are interested in men and this makes the problems . . . problems for the girls anyway. For the man it is a very nice situation in England.

'Not only are they doing it all the time, they are talking about it all the time. Whether they're enjoying the doing I'm not so sure, I think maybe they are enjoying more the talking *about* than the doing.'

INGRID: (*Swedish*)

I am very surprised that Englishmen prefer a lot of rugs and warm water bottles in their beds instead of some more pleasant form of heating. I had only seen English men on films and on the television and they were always with the bowling hats and the umbrellas and everything like that, and no smiles. But they're not like that, they're not like the men I saw on the television. I thought really everyone would be like that man in *The Avengers*. But then, maybe if I go to America I would expect everyone on a horse.

LILI: (*Austrian*)

The trouble with the English male is that he didn't evolve, he had a revolution. Suddenly they have become attractive, the most attractive men in the world.

ROSANNA: (*Italian*)

Everyone in England is a hypocrite except for George Brown.

EVA: (*Danish*)

I have met English women who have admitted killing their husbands. Yes, killing them with pastries, with cakes, with biscuits, with stuffing them to death.

ROSANNA: (*Italian*)

They don't know what clean is. To clean under things, to clean in corners, to clean behind things, they don't bother with this. They just want lots of polish around. It became enough for me to just open up a tin of polish so that the room smelled properly. This is my dishonest point, but if I didn't feel like cleaning the room it was enough to just put some *smell* of polish around and then the lady would say 'Oh isn't it nice and clean in here'. Believe me, you go look on top of English wardrobes, behind English sofas, under English beds, and you will find enough dirt to plant a beautiful garden in. Believe me.

JULIE: (*American*)

Yes, the dirt here is pretty upsetting at first. When I had to go out and buy carrots and potatoes I'd get pretty disturbed about it, because there was so much dried mud all over them, and they'd just dump them in your shopping bag. However, I accustomed myself to that. But then, you know, I got this terrible habit over here. It's a habit of looking in people's ears. What I mean is if I get on a bus or I'm standing in a queue somewhere, I just *have* to look into people's ears, because I want to find out just how much wax and dirt and general refuse the English are carrying around in their ears. I know it's a sick habit but it started when I was in the subway in the rush hour, and it stopped with a big bump, and I found myself looking straight into someone's ear. And *wow*, I never saw so much wax in my life. Well, I became fascinated by this, almost obsessed, and honestly after six months of looking into ears I think the English really do have more wax in their ears than they do on their furniture.

CATHERINE: (*Dutch*)

The English male is over-sexed, this is only a general theory.

MASHIE: (*Yugoslavian*)

Very very nice, very nice like Prince Philip.

INGRID: (*Swedish*)

Maybe you can understand older people, middle-aged people

being interested in orgies, but here young people do them. They are the boy's fault, because the girl thinks she is going to a nice party, and all the boys have been getting together and getting ready for an orgy.

Lena: (*Polish*)

You can't easy tell who is the Jews here.

Eva: (*Danish*)

The Latin Americans and the Continentals talk and talk about love but he doesn't do anything about it. The Englishman doesn't talk, he just does it. The Latin sees himself as the most important sexual animal, takes himself so seriously. Well, the Englishman just laughs at the whole idea, at the *idea* of himself being the great lover, so a girl is apt not to think of him as very serious, or very dangerous. But I warn them, that the Englishman may not *talk* about sex much, but he really means business.

Ingrid: (*Swedish*)

If you are young this is the only place to be, but if you are over twenty-two or so maybe it's not so good.

Julie: (*American*)

To me the funniest thing is this big split between the young and the kind of forty-year-olds, I mean in fashion. The mothers all seem to go round in these little satin hats, and pearls, and muskrat stoles, and at the same time their kids are going around with their skirts up to their belly buttons and their hair below them, and there just doesn't seem to be any kind of visual relationship between them. In America we don't have these extreme contrasts. Girls try to dress upwards, towards the way their mothers do, and the mothers do the same thing in reverse.

MARIANNE: (*Swiss*)

You might call it Swinging London, but maybe this is very old fashioned, but I think it is a degenerating thing. What's swinging, what's even happy about sleeping in the streets, living together when you're only fifteen or sixteen, starving yourself so you can buy drugs? And this is the crowd that people call Swinging London. Some of them, their lives are finished before they're even seventeen.

CARMEN: (*Spanish*)

The police here are very kind. In Spain you are always a bit scared of them, because they will put you in clink first then maybe solve your problem after. Here it is the other way around, they solve your problem first so then they don't have to put you in clink, and I think they are like friends to me.

CATHERINE: (*Dutch*)

The English seem to be very tolerant but this is just their laziness. 'We don't care about anything,' they say, 'so let them do what they like'. So they don't care enough about anything really to be *in*tolerant.

MARIANNE: (*Swiss*)

I have never known English girls to have *real* girl friends. You know, to confide in each other, and to trust each other. All the girls are terribly lonely, and they only consider their girl friends as rivals who want to take their boy friends away. And they are quite right, which makes it even worse. I've seen this, if one girl has a boy friend every other girl is chasing that boy and is trying to take him away. This attitude that girls can't trust each other even when they're sharing the same flat is dreadful. Of course they want someone to love, to be loved, someone to care for, and of course they want to get married, but the English girl gets so desperate for these things that she will try to chase any boy away from any girl. It is only in this country that I have seen this, definitely. I have been watching at clubs and it's dreadful that any man, *any* man can walk up to any girl and get her. Whether he's married or not it doesn't matter, she's longing for someone so much she doesn't care. I don't blame the English man for this, if he can get something so easily why shouldn't he? It is the girl's fault. They are all so afraid, I don't know why. And these girls are so obvious in the way they show they *are* desperate. A European woman has much more pride you know. The English girl doesn't care what the man is like, whether they have anything to say to each other. To her it is just bed bed bed . . . whether it's for a night, a week, or a month, she just takes anything that comes along.

LILI: (*Austrian*)

If a girl wants to have fun she should go away from London and go to the farther cities like Birmingham and Glasgow. In London there are too many homosexuals. There are not so many in the other places, I think because they all have come to London.

MARIANNE: (*Swiss*)

The separate schools make all this happen. When they are separated they get so obsessed with sex, it's not natural for boys not having girls around them all the time. If a boy is having girls around him all the time, just as friends, just there, they are cooling down, they stop wanting just to jump into bed with the first girl they meet. They feel they can pick and choose, they don't worry about the whole *idea* of sex so much. But here they feel they *should* go to bed with a girl when they are only fourteen, and it's just like smoking with them, just to experiment with being adult. This unnatural thing of being kept away from girls makes them obsessed with ' doing it '. That's what they call sex, ' doing *it* ', as if ' it ' was the only thing in their lives. Dreadful.

Catherine: (*Dutch*)

I have seen with my own boy friend and with my friends who have married English men, that he will stay a mother's son first, and a wife's husband second.

Rosanna: (*Italian*)

I married one, and to me he is the only *real* man in the world.

Dominique: (*French*)

They don't take it for normal to drink wine at home, excepting when there are special guests. Then they will go out and buy expensive bad wine instead of cheap good wine. And they are so funny, they make such a fuss over this bad wine, tasting and smelling and talking about it, so serious about the wine instead of just drinking it. They are really better with their beer.

Rosanna: (*Italian*)

I think they go to the pubs so much just to be warm. I don't think anyone would go to an English pub for any other kind of pleasure.

Lili: (*Austrian*)

They pile up little statues and bits of silver and glass and pictures and plants and bits of china and they put them all over the room and say ' There isn't that cosy?' And you want to say ' No, it is *freezing*!'

MARLENE: (*German*)

It is to me just a part of their character. They are so cold inside that they don't notice the cold outside, they are against *any* kind of warmth.

ROSANNA: (*Italian*)

They are cold inside. They just *say* ' darling, darling '. Even the window cleaner calls you ' darling ' and it doesn't mean anything.

CATHERINE: (*Dutch*)

They have been locked up all their lives in their boarding schools, in their grammar schools, locked away from girls, then when they are allowed loose, they just go wild. I have been to a students' party at Oxford and I am not prudish but it was really horrible. When each girl arrived she would just be matched off with a boy, with someone she had never seen before, and told ' You go with him '. And there were mattresses all over the floor, and people made love, just next to each other. I got violently sick, and they let me leave, but this was these boys' idea of an enjoyable party.

INGRID: (*Swedish*)

To me a boy or a man is nothing special, there are hundreds of them around, they are basically the same, they all got the same things, they all want the same things. Okay? Maybe I am the same too.

'Even the window cleaner calls you "darling" and it doesn't mean anything'

But to an English girl, when she meets a boy she gets so excited, she treats him as if he wasn't even another human being, like he had dropped down from the sky. And she starts running around like an idiot for him. She is waiting for him to say 'Jump' and up she goes, she is waiting for him to say 'Down' and down she goes, and she is hoping he will say 'Bed', and then in she goes. She's stupid.

I know Swedish girls are very popular here and everyone thinks it is because we go to bed with boys but this is not true, not true at all. Because we have been brought up with boys and have gone to school with boys we can talk to boys like our friends. So the English boys bring us their problems to talk about. That is why they like us, not for sex, because they get all the sex they want from English girls.

You see, we learn everything about sex at school. Since I was four years old, five years old I have been learning everything about sex. And we learn there is nothing dirty. Nothing to be feeling nasty about. So if a boy wants, and I want, we go to bed. If I don't want . . . no we don't. But I am not saying 'Yes' always to anyone. But the English girl is saying 'Yes' to nearly any man and then worrying 'Oh, what would my mother think, my aunt, my cousin, my grandmother . . . what would they think if they knew what a dirty thing I have done'. *And* they don't know how to do it, *and* they don't use contraceptives, *and* they get babies.

CLAUDE: (*Belgian*)

The babies are beautiful, but the children are terrible. I used to take the little baby out in the pram, and the dog, a Corgi I think you call it, was tied to the pram with a long strap, and everyone would stop and say 'Oh lovely dog, isn't he nice?' and no one would ever look at the baby. And I said to the mother 'I am going to put the baby on the strap one day because I think she needs some attention also', but the mother didn't laugh.

35

INGRID: (*Swedish*)

If you are brought up right about sex you know what to say to a boy, and if you don't want the boy you just keep on saying ' No ', and if you keep on saying ' No ' the boy can't get it up and if he can't get it up he can't get on. That's true isn't it? But the English girl she never learned to say ' No '.

She has never learned anything really about sex. English boys have told me that the English girls don't know anything about sex the first time, that they have to have everything explained to them the first time, and then it has to be explained again during. Well if you know boys you know they don't have that much time to be explaining during.

But all this is so new to the English girl that sex becomes very important to her and she tries to tie herself tight to any man who has gone to bed with her, she don't know how to say to a man ' Okay, that was nice, thank you – finished, goodbye '. Maybe it isn't her fault. She is not taught to know what she wants, so it's easy for a boy to tell her that what she wants is what *he* wants, and she don't really get much pleasure from it, well the boys say that, I don't know. Anyway she starts worrying right away ' Does he think I'm dirty? Does he think I'm horrible?' Maybe she is right, because it *is* dirty and horrible to go to bed with a man you don't really want.

LENA: (*Polish*)

You can't easy tell who is the Jews here.

INGRID: (*Swedish*)

But I don't think the English girl wants any *special* man, she just wants *a* man, *any* man . . . and when she is invited out to the cinema her mind is already jumping ahead to the church. So maybe here is the trouble, the English girl is never a girl, she is always almost a wife.

36

'You can't easy tell who is the Jews here'

CARMEN: (*Spanish*)

They are not mothers. They let the schools, and the nurse-maids and the au-pairs do their mothers' job.

INGRID: (*Swedish*)

And the English boy, like all boys, don't think he's almost a husband.

But the English boy is more male than the Swedish boy . . . and more a gentleman too, he opens doors, pays for everything, and he seems very respectful. But when he wants sex he is not too respectful, but this is male too. If you say ' No ', he is okay, he isn't angry, and if you say ' Yes ', I have found they are not too precipitate, either before or during sex. They are really quite good, and I often wonder where they learned to be so good in bed, because I don't think that they learned this from English girls.

CATHERINE: (*Dutch*)

The English girl sticks to her boy friend like a fly sticks to honey. You see them walking in the street, the girl hanging on to the boy friend's arm, looking up at him, trying desperately to get his attention, she is weighing him down like an anchor. At the age of eighteen she is already worried about being a spinster.

INGRID: (*Swedish*)

But, to end, I would say I wouldn't take an English boy for a husband, because I think they are too sure of being men that they wouldn't make good husbands, but I think they are very nice without marriage, and I hope English girls learn more soon.

MARLENE: (*German*)

From the German point of view the English women are very bad housekeepers. They are mean, very mean. They don't want to spend money. They spend the smallest amounts on food and on heating. In Germany the family money always goes *first* for food, for heat, for comfort at home. Then if anything is left over maybe we buy new curtains, new wallpaper. Here they buy first for showing off to other people, and what is left over is spent on food and heat for the family. No, they are really mean. They will make their families shiver and starve to have new curtains in the front window.

ROSANNA: (*Italian*)

They say that women are the same the world over, but I think the Englishwoman is less so. I have never heard in any place so many women who like to talk about cooking. And on the radio and on the television there are many many programmes about cooking, and there are the magazines and the newspapers with beautiful pictures and beautiful recipes, and every woman has this vast library of cooking books. And all of this talk and looking and listening and discussing produces –

DOMINIQUE: (*French*)

Petit pois à la menthe, les légumes à l'eau, le rôti brûlé. It is terrible.

LENA: (*Polish*)

I don't complain. No one is starving.

MARIANNE: (*Swiss*)

But when you see the slums here it is as if it was Dickens. I have seen how many people live here. Toilets in the backyard, no hot water, no baths, mice running in rubbish, children running around in torn clothes and dirt all over them, not like the way children get dirty, but like children who are never, *never* washed. And you see women walking around without stockings and their legs covered with mud up to the knees, all spattered from the rain, but you know that it hasn't been raining for two days.

JULIE: (*American*)

You'll really think this is stupid, or at any rate naïve, but when I first started travelling around, just looking at places you know, I just couldn't get over the number of public baths you had, particularly in the slummy places. And I thought, ' This is a great thing. A sea-faring people, so they're all learning to swim '. Then when I discovered that your Public Baths weren't swimming baths but like baths where you went to get clean I felt really disillusioned. I just cannot believe that some people don't have bathrooms of their own.

MARIANNE: (*Swiss*)

They *are* dirty, they *do* smell. But if you have no hot water in the house, if you have to go into a cold backyard to wash yourself, then you wash yourself less. So if people smell on the tube, everywhere, I don't blame them. I mean in Switzerland the first thing a labourer does when he comes home is to have a shower, or a bath, change his clothes. But here they come home dirty, and go to bed dirty, because of the English housing and sanitary fitments. But still, they do smell.

LENA: (*Polish*)

The streets are swept clean, and everyone is so precise about putting their litter into the baskets, and no one spits, so I think it is pretty clean, outside anyway.

MASHIE: (*Yugoslavian*)

The best part is London parks. There is no signs saying 'Keep Off the Grass' and people can eat on it and boys and girls make love there. I like this very much.

ROSANNA: (*Italian*)

Of course you have freedom of speech here but I think that this is because most of the time no one is really listening to you.

INGRID: (*Swedish*)

They never mean what they say. They have been taught to be like this when they are very very young, that they must say 'Hello, nice to see you', even if they hate the people, and I think it is awful. You see, in Swedish schools we learn that you must be very honest and direct with other people, that you should not lie about being friendly, and that you must be your own personality to please *you*, not to please other people. I have learned also Shakespeare and 'To thine own self be true' but I think most English people have never learnt this, or maybe they forgot it.

JULIE: (*American*)

You have a marvellous educational system here, but I don't think you really appreciate it.

LILI: (*Austrian*)

The trouble is a boy here feels he has been kept apart from girls like they were both some animals in a zoo, wild wild animals, and when they meet they have nothing shared in common, nothing to talk about, and it seems to these poor children that the only way they can have something in common is to go to bed.

CARMEN: (*Spanish*)

In Spain, I never went anywhere without my mother or older sister as chaperone, and I didn't like it at all. But now I am here, and I see what English girls do, and that boys have no respect for these girls, well I am glad that I was brought up strict. Here everything is too loose.

LENA: (*Polish*)

If you have been brought up strict the whole place makes you dizzy.

JULIE: (*American*)

Of course I'd read about the whole scene before I came over, and I guess I'd visualized it, sort of fantasized it, the whole thing going on with me right in the middle, and of course in my experience it's just been a big bust. I mean this swinging London scene was created by a bunch of rich people, you just think of all those Lords This and Lady Thats who run the boutiques and the little clubs and so on . . . right? Well they're raking in money and having a ball, and the general run of poor kid is spinning around in a kind of frenzy trying to keep up with something that was created for other people. So lots of people are making lots of profit out of it but to me it's just a big racket.

CLAUDE: (*Belgian*)

How can London swing when the buses stop before midnight?

KARIN: (*Norwegian*)

In Soho they will try to drug your drinks and drag you away. I don't blame these experiences on the English but because there are so many foreigners there.

MASHIE: (*Yugoslavian*)

I think the best thing is for you all to come and have holiday in my country.

DOMINIQUE: (*French*)

No money? No pleasure. That is London.

LILI: (*Austrian*)

England is not a country for the future, not even for the present, you are looking for your past, always admiring your past.

CARMEN: (*Spanish*)

They are cold, sad and lonely.

MARIANNE: (*Swiss*)

In a tube wagon here there is complete silence. Everyone is hiding behind their paper afraid to talk to each other. Sometimes I think you buy so many newspapers here not to read them but to use them like a shield. When the paper goes up in the front of the face it is like a signal to other people, ' I am not really here, so don't, please don't look at me, please don't talk to me, please don't bother me '. And sometimes I wonder if you stopped selling newspapers in this country if the people would all go crazy, because then they might really *have* to look at each other and *think* about each other and I think they would go crazy.

JULIE: (*American*)

I think there is this very definite fear here of blundering into the wrong class, and this may inhibit some people from making new friends. I've seen this in my suburb, that if you invite the A's who are (perhaps) lower middle class, you're putting yourself down one rung in the ladder. That's bad enough, but if you invite the B's who *appear* to be upper middle class, you're running the risk of being turned down, and made to feel really inferior, and that's even worse. Of course the whole thing is really sick, because no one knows who is really what any more and who cares? Except the English *do* care.

ROSANNA: (*Italian*)

Everyone in England is a hypocrite except for George Brown.

EVA: (*Danish*)

They are not flexible. England is like a statue that gets a little chip here, some moss goes there, dirt makes it look black, but the stone underneath doesn't change. And it doesn't even know it's got bird dirt on its head.

INGRID: (*Swedish*)

They think that being born as speaking English means that no other language is important.

DOMINIQUE: (*French*)

You don't *like* us . . . we don't *need* you.

ROSANNA: (*Italian*)

The worst is the English coming back from holiday. I say, for God's sake if you go to Italy don't send back postcards saying 'The water gives me stomach ache, the food is too greasy, the sun is too hot, the men are too rude, the rooms are too dirty', and then come back and right away start planning your *next* year's holiday in Italy! Why go back if it causes you so much pain?

CATHERINE: (*Dutch*)

The first time I went into a lavatory on an English train I really couldn't believe what I was seeing. I really couldn't believe I was still in a civilized country.

DOMINIQUE: (*French*)

But no one tries to take advantage of you here. If you give too much money they run after you to return the money. Even the cab drivers will do this, and this would never happen in Paris.

INGRID: (*Swedish*)

I like the markets in the streets.

JULIE: (*American*)

I had a wisdom tooth out and it cost me nothing. Back home it would have been fifty dollars at least.

EVA: (*Danish*)

Every garden has a rose, this is lovely. So are the pubs.

DOMINIQUE: (*French*)

I think everything *looks* very exciting. The young people dress in this very individual way, they are very colourful, very dramatic, and when you first see all these people it is very exciting. But then you find out that they really only appear to be this way. I think they spend so much time, and money, and thought, and passion on the way they are *looking*, that they have nothing left over for being, for doing.

CLAUDE: (*Belgian*)

The English girl has a very sweet voice, very soft, very pretty, but she never have much to say with it.

CATHERINE: (*Dutch*)

I think your early marriage is a very bad habit because these people are too young to be good mothers and fathers to their children.

CATHERINE: (*Dutch*)

I think there is a very distinct difference between the attitude of the upper classes and the middle classes towards their children. I see the working people really very fond of each other, interested in each other, and I think this is because there is not so much money and they have had a struggle to bring their children up. I think this struggle makes for stronger ties in the family. If you are upper class and you send your son to boarding school, all you must do is write up a cheque. But the working class here has to all work together and plan together to keep their son on at grammar school.

MASHIE: (*Yugoslavian*)

In my country we think all children are interesting, in your country you think all children are boring. Maybe you make them boring.

ROSANNA: (*Italian*)

I think English women have their children, bring them up to the age of school –

Ingrid: (*Swedish*)

If I had to wear those awful uniforms I would have left school when I was twelve.

Rosanna: (*Italian*)

– and then . . . phwee . . . they wash their hands of them. They're out. It is the teacher's job to bring them up. And then, then when they are sixteen, it's either you have studied and earned your university or you go out and get a job. They don't actually push them out of the house, they don't *throw* them out, oh no, but it is ' You give me part of your wages ' and ' Don't expect *me* to wash your clothes '. And suddenly, so suddenly to this sixteen-year-old, Mother doesn't exist any more. This is true even in the best families, yes, even in Catholic families. The mother thinks ' Well, I have done my duty, I have produced these children, now it is finished '. Now, as an Italian, I think my duty only will *begin* when I am in labour with my child, and this duty and this love must continue through all your life, so you can always give your children the right things that they need. But the English deny this real love, and doing this hurts everybody, the children and the parents, and it really hurts *me* to see this kind of coldness in the English family. I think all of them need some kissing, some hugging, even the grown-ups need this.

Marlene: (*German*)

They are never very happy and they are never very sad. I think if there was a disaster they would just go on with their lives, smiling and being polite, and not really thinking or feeling too much about the disaster. It is very peculiar. I know the English say that the Germans are too serious but I think it is much better to feel *something* – to either weep or to laugh than to be like the English, always living in the middle.

47

DOMINIQUE: (*French*)

They're not really against anything because they're not really *for* anything.

ROSANNA: (*Italian*)

Look, how can they do anything? They don't even join up with each other. The North here don't like the South here, and the other way round. So how are they going to join up with anything else? With Europe? Never! First they must learn to give, then maybe they will get. But by the time they learn to give it will probably be too late to get anything back from the rest of the world.

MARLENE: (*German*)

They are like a Polo mint. Very sweet and smooth on the outside, but inside there is nothing at all.

EVA: (*Danish*)

They *think* they have friends but I don't think this is true. They just collect acquaintances. The main thing seems to be to know many people, but when they are with these people there is nothing that really connects them. They never talk to each other about what they are thinking or feeling, just about business and the weather and everyday things.

MARLENE: (*German*)

It is not social and it is not family. When you come into an English house the family is always sitting around the telly, not even around the chimney piece. In Germany it would be different.

MASHIE: (*Yugoslavian*)

I think the best thing is for you all to come and have holiday in my country.

CATHERINE: (*Dutch*)

Why should they belong anywhere except here? They know they are born on an island, then his family teaches him to believe that the family and the family house is an island, and finally he himself becomes an island. Perhaps they are happy that way, they have never known anything else.

EVA: (*Danish*)

If only they still did not think of all foreigners as bloody wogs.

ROSANNA: (*Italian*)

The Italians are very famous for being dirty, the English think. And they think they are so clean here, and everything for the baby must be boiled, they would boil the baby if the doctor told them to. But at the same time while they are sterilizing everything, you can go into the lavatory and oh, it smells beautifully of Harpic, but when you wash your hands the towel is filthy, and there is always dirt around the taps of English wash basins.

CLAUDE: (*Belgian*)

An English housewife is only cleaning on the surface. Once a week she is polishing the silver and putting it on show, and there are cobwebs hanging from the ceiling.

CATHERINE: (*Dutch*)

I disagree. The English wife is a slave. The husband is waited on hand and foot, and never helps the wife around the house.

I don't honestly think the husband *does* more in Holland, it's just that the wife *complains* more.

JULIE: (*American*)

Considering the amount of domestic help she gets, the English woman still seems awfully tied to the house. I guess this really applies to the middle class but that's all I know about here. I mean in our suburb everyone seems to have an au-pair and a lot of them a daily cleaner as well, but the women themselves still seem to be all tied up in their domestic routine. There is nothing to stop them from going out and doing new things, and meeting new people, and having a little fun for themselves, but they seem to prefer staying at home all the time, and complaining about the fact that they *do* stay at home all the time. Middle-class martyred moms . . . they're a sort of cop-out from any kind of challenge.

CATHERINE: (*Dutch*)

Once they have a child they are *so* relieved, and they say 'Well now I am a *Mother* so I can give everything else up'. They have no emancipation at all. I do not understand them.

EVA: (*Danish*)

In my mind I see the English mother in a little cage, and I don't really see where her windows are. She doesn't really want to have anything to *do* with her children. When he's small her idea of a relationship with him is to give him a piece of candy to keep him quiet. Then, when he gets too big, and he comes to her and asks questions, questions that she finds too difficult to answer, or she won't take time to deal with them, she just sends him away to boarding school. And he comes home as a perfect polite little stranger who will shake hands with his parents and call his father ' sir '. So his mother has managed to put her children into cages too.

MARIANNE: (*Swiss*)

They don't make real homes here. They don't share things, help each other, don't let the children participate in the home, they don't make the effort of being *friendly* with their children.

LILI: (*Austrian*)

How can they be good mothers when they are afraid to be cross with their children? Or they are too lazy to be cross with them. If you love your children and you want what is good for them, you must be cross with them at times. I see how badly the children behave here, and it's difficult for me to watch because the mother is just saying 'Oh sweetie you shouldn't do this! Oh darling don't do that! Sweetie you'll break it! Darling do be good!' . . . and the children are just going ahead and being naughty. They are not listening to the mothers. These words are not meaning anything. 'Darling' doesn't mean anything here. If I say this word in German it is 'Liebling', and if I say this I really *mean* it, and I am not saying it to a child every day. So the mothers do not mean what they are saying, the children know they don't mean what they are saying, and the mothers are driving their children crazy.

ROSANNA: (*Italian*)

At the age of two it is 'Don't do this, don't do that'. They must sit properly at the table, sit properly on the potty, they must be fully trained like they were little performing animals in circuses. But we believe let the child do what he wants, take all the damages away before he can get to them, but the children must be let to go, to enjoy, to *live*! Here everyone is frightened they will spoil their children, but they don't understand, that love, *real* love cannot spoil anything, only *pretending* to love can spoil.

CATHERINE: (*Dutch*)

I don't care what you are served in restaurants, what happens outside the home. It is *inside* the home where food really matters. And inside the home they are very bad for two reasons. First they are lazy, they won't spend time on making good food, and second they will *not* try anything new. They don't want adventure in their cooking. Roasts, stews and potatoes, that's what they want, and let the restaurants give them 'special' foods. They have no fantasy about food.

EVA: (*Danish*)

The English woman's idea of a salad is a piece of dead lettuce, a bit of mashed up beetroot and half a rotten tomato.

JULIE: (*American*)

It's really pretty hard to believe that there is any relationship between those great vegetables you see in the shops and on the stalls and the mess that is served up as 'veg' on the dining table.

KARIN: (*Norwegian*)

They don't know that if food is pleasing to the eye it tastes better. But sometimes I think the English don't really care about the look or the taste, they just want to feel stuffed up. Think of mash and bangers.

CARMEN: (*Spanish*)

You see they think it is enough to put some kind of a meal on the table. Then they are cooks. Well that's what they think. But I know if their families had to eat the food the way it was bought in the stores they would end up with fresh-frozen stomachs.

JULIE: (*American*)

I have to admit that I think there is more flavour to the food here than back home, but it isn't served prettily. There's no effort made to use a little garnish you know, and you can lose your appetite just by looking at it.

DOMINIQUE: (*French*)

Oh it makes me feel ill to talk about it. To me it has been like watching a terrible murder three times a day.

CARMEN: (*Spanish*)

Don't blame the women, blame the men. It is the men who make English cooking so bad. If the wife puts garlic in they say 'Uggh what is this?' If she makes a sauce he says 'Good meat doesn't need this muck'. If she tries something new that he has never eaten he says, 'I'm not hungry, I'll just have some eggs'. If she make a nice steak he says 'Oh I had steak for lunch' and if she don't make a nice steak he says 'Why don't we ever have steak? Don't I give you enough housekeeping money?' And if she would give him roast beef, potatoes, peas and cabbage every day he would say 'Oh you *are* a good cook'. So he is to blame, he doesn't get bored with the same thing day after day, but the poor wife does, and she gives up, so she never learns to cook.

DOMINIQUE: (*French*)

I can't say I find him at all interesting. He doesn't understand women, and I am not interested in anyone who doesn't understand *me*. I understand *him*, of course, but that is not really enough is it?

CARMEN: (*Spanish*)

I think in a way this makes the English man more attractive.

53

DOMINIQUE: (*French*)

He comes home and eats everything up. Then he watches the television and then he says ' Well, I'll be off now ' and he goes to bed. He never talks to his wife. If she tries to make a conversation with him he says ' Oh please, I'm very tired, I've been talking all day '. In this country I think marriage is only a convenience to a man.

EVA: (*Danish*)

He is good at making fires, good at making a cup of tea, he is good in bed, but as a soul-mate he is non-existent.

JULIE: (*American*)

I never feel they're really relaxed with me. There's always this kind of strain.

MARIANNE: (*Swiss*)

They are very *internal* people. Now they don't fight outside their country they fight each other. And they are so busy worrying about what they think of each other that they have no time to worry about what the rest of the world thinks of them.

MARLENE: (*German*)

It is not their fault that they won't belong. It is the way they are brought up. They are told that it is good to get something without working hard for it. So they are lazy. They have not learned to like work because work is good. And no one wants lazy people as their comrades.

CLAUDE: (*Belgian*)

The English man is very selfish . . . well any man is selfish . . .

probably every human being is selfish . . . but the English man is worse because he is not even *ashamed* of being selfish. He believes this is his natural role in life. He believes that women should worship him, all girls admire him, he thinks that he shouldn't have to bother in trying to get a girl, he should just wait until they fall for him – and the funny thing is they *do*!

ROSANNA: (*Italian*)

Everyone in England is a hypocrite except for George Brown.

The Cast

CLAUDE: (*Belgian*)

Claude is nineteen. She comes from a small town near Ostend. She was part of a large family, the oldest child of nine, and when she was sixteen her mother threw her out. Why this happened Claude will not say. She has been in England for over sixteen months, and has been with five families, all of whom have repeated the previous family pattern. 'They throw me out. I don't see why, there seems no rest for a person like me.' And you *don't* see why. She seems capable, a sturdy, self-possessed, rather squat little person. Before she came to England she was in France, where she worked as a chamber maid in Nimes, then in Marseilles. She has the hands of a middle-aged woman.

MASHIE: (*Yugoslavian*)

Mashie is twenty. She is devoted to her country and to the *idea* of her country. She wants to perfect her English so that she can join the Yugoslavian Tourist Board. She is a very shiny girl, hair, teeth, eyes, shoes, nails, all are glossy and sparkling. When she understands your question she nods and smiles, and when she doesn't understand your question she nods and smiles. She is terribly anxious that everyone she meets in England should like her. 'Not to like *me*, but to like a *Yugoslavian*, then maybe everyone I meet will come and have holiday in my country.' She has been here for ten months.

DOMINIQUE: (*French*)

Dominique is twenty-one, but projects an air of such languid elegance that she appears much older. She seems to be much given to black fox, green eyeshadow, and stumpy heels. She comes from Lyons where her father is a mathematics teacher. She first went to Paris for a year, where she worked as a receptionist for 'someone very famous'. She came here a year ago and has had six different au-pair jobs during that time. She doesn't blame the families but herself. 'I should never have become an au-pair, I don't like washing other people's dirty dishes'. She seemed rather disinterested in both the questions asked and the answers given. She finds England 'without intellectual conversation'. She never smiles, but makes use of her eyebrows to convey her rather limited moods.

Eva: (*Danish*)

Eva is twenty-two. She came to England three years ago, first to work as an au-pair for a Cambridge professor and his family, then in London. She had taken one year of English Studies at university in Denmark, before she and her family decided that the idea of au-pair was appealing to all. Her father is a bank manager ('but only a tiny branch') and her mother 'writes some poetry'. She is engaged to be married to an Englishman, whom she met when she was in Cambridge as an au-pair and he as a student. She is an original, and can wear a tweed cape, thigh-high boots, leather shorts (yes, *shorts*) and a big grin, without the slightest sign of self-consciousness.

Carmen: (*Spanish*)

Carmen is twenty-three. She comes from the north of Spain, from an upper middle-class family. Her father was the mayor of the town for ten years. 'Next to the Duke we are the most important family in the town'. She is tiny, only five feet tall, and it is disconcerting to hear her very loud husky voice emerging from such a small frame. She is agile in action and in thought, dark and pretty. When we met she was actually wearing a black satin rose behind one ear. She has been here for two years, has worked with seven different families. She is happy, finally, with her present family because 'They keep *proper* servants in the house, and I am no longer treated like a slave'.

Julie: (*American*)

Until I met Julie I didn't even know there was such a thing as an American au-pair. She is twenty-one, didn't come to study the language, but has discovered 'There's American English and English English, and I'm still learning'. She comes from a suburb outside Chicago. 'We're pretty prosperous, three cars and a hired maid for cocktail parties'. She took two years of sociology at a State University before she got 'hung up' and her parents felt that a year away from home and the home country might help her. What the 'hang up' was about she doesn't say, but there were hints of a quiet abortion. Since she has been here she has worked for two families. The first family had been contacted through a lawyer friend of her father's, and she didn't feel happy there because she believed that 'reports about Julie might be flying back and forth across the Atlantic'. She got her present job through a local employment agency. She is bright, a little brash, not particularly pretty, and is apt to drop into 'hip' talk to hide any emotion.

LILI: (*Austrian*)

Lili is twenty-three. She comes from Vienna where her widowed mother is a part-time dressmaker. Before her father died he was a machine engineer. Lili had high hopes of becoming a great ski champion, but has settled for a future of being a hotel-receptionist-cum-ski-instructor. In order to do this she needs at least four languages, and before coming here she spent a year in Paris and a year in Milan to perfect her French and Italian. She has been here for two years, and admits ' My English was fine a year ago, I'd passed my Cambridge Efficiency, but when the time came I didn't want to go, so I just stayed '. She is a giggler, an enthusiast, and quite astonishingly attractive. She once went skiing in Scotland, and still finds the fact hard to believe.

Marlene: (*German*)

Marlene is twenty-one, and she worked for two years as a secretary in Germany. She is vague about her family background, except to say that she comes from ' North Germany, the forest lands '. She has worked for two families since coming here eighteen months ago, and both families lived in the country, one in Cornwall, the other in Dorset. She was very precise about everything. Handbag and gloves to be arranged in a definite order, every cigarette stubbed out three times, her feet, once crossed, remained crossed. Her answers were slow to be made. When she did speak she spoke carefully, but without hesitation. She had many opinions, but seemed curiously remote from them, as if everything she had experienced here had happened to someone else.

Ingrid: (*Swedish*)

Ingrid is eighteen and has been here for only three months. She was fired from her first job (for staying out too late), and was living at a Swedish hostel when I met her. She comes from a small industrial town situated north-west of Stockholm. Her father is a die-maker for the railroads, and she has three younger sisters. Her spoken English is very good, but she can't write in English. She admits, with an honesty calculated to be refreshing, that she did *not* come here to perfect her English but to have fun. She is having fun, day and night, and her English is obviously being enriched, though much of the enrichment is not publishable. She is five feet two, pretty the way a mink is pretty, with sharp little teeth, bright avid eyes, and a tiny twitching nose. She is completely honest and endearing, but not, from the employer's point of view, the ideal au-pair.

MARIANNE: (*Swiss*)

Marianne is twenty-five. She lives in a town about thirty miles from Zurich. Her father is an executive in a large Swiss company, her mother is a housewife. Marianne describes them both as ' conservative but kind '. She was trained as a teacher and taught primary school classes for two years before leaving Switzerland to come here as au-pair. She studied English for two years here, and has just taken up a post as a teacher in a London secondary school. Before becoming an au-pair she worked for six months as an Assistant Matron in an English boarding school. Those six months she says, ' have coloured all my opinions about England, because it is in a second rate boarding school that you see all that is bad and brutal about Britain '. Despite the badness and the brutality, she married a product of the English boarding school system a few months ago, and intends to spend the rest of her life in this country.

CATHERINE: (*Dutch*)

Catherine is only nineteen but has the composure of a woman twice her age. She comes from Amsterdam and has been au-pair here for almost two years. During that time she has worked for ten different families. She doesn't blame herself for all the changing about, but the families. She wanted to go to university in Holland, but there wasn't enough money, so au-pairing was felt to be the next best thing. Catherine has no plans at all for the future. She feels, ' Maybe coming here and learning so much in every way when you are only seventeen makes you frightened to think of what may be happening to you next year, or even tomorrow. So now I don't think, I just keep on being au-pair, like I am trapped in being au-pair '. It may sound like a Rapunzel in need of a rescuer, but as Catherine is six feet tall, and very assured with it, the romance doesn't quite fit the reality.

ROSANNA: (*Italian*)

Rosanna is twenty-eight and has been in England for almost seven years. She has been married to an English man for a year, and now lives in a town some forty miles from London. She worked for so many families during her au-pair years that she has lost track of the number. ' No, I have never counted them all up, there are too many . . . maybe twenty, thirty, I don't know '. She is very excitable and punctuates everything with magnificently extravagant gestures. When she is really agitated she has a habit of leaning over and pinching your upper arm. This grip is held until you nod to assure her that you've understood what she's trying to explain. Then you are momentarily released. She was beautifully dressed and groomed, and in a daze of contentment about the fact that she is having her first baby in five months. When Rosanna says 'It will be the most beautiful baby in the world', you believe her.

KARIN: (*Norwegian*)

Karin is twenty. She comes from a large family in the south of Norway. They are farmers but 'not peasants, we are really quite wealthy'. She has been an au-pair here for three months with one family, and she says she is very happy with her position. She plans to go to France at the end of her year here and then to New York to become an interpreter at the United Nations. She takes her English studies very seriously, as indeed she takes most things. She has to take pills every four hours, 'For anxiety, the doctor says. This illness only came to me since I have been here'.

LENA: (*Polish*)

Lena is very proud to be one of the first au-pairs to come here from Poland. Of all the girls she seemed the most foreign, perhaps because she was quite peculiarly dressed in a style that could only be described as hand-crocheted. Even her shoes and stockings looked as if they'd just been run up that morning. She is only allowed, as a Pole, to stay here for one year and will be returning to Warsaw in three months. Her father is a dentist and her mother runs a 'little shop that sells many kind of little things'. Lena trained as an accountant, but didn't like it, and now wants to be an official interpreter.

The Library of

Crosby Hall